The GI in Combat
Northwest Europe 1944-45

Text by Steven J. Zaloga
Color plates by Ronald B. Volstad

D1709787

Copyright © 2002
by CONCORD PUBLICATIONS CO.
603-609 Castle Peak Road
Kong Nam Industrial Building
10/F, B1, Tsuen Wan
New Territories, Hong Kong
www.concord-publications.com

We welcome authors who can help
expand our range of books. If you
would like to submit material,
please feel free to contact us.

We are always on the look-out for new,
unpublished photos for this series.
If you have photos or slides or
information you feel may be useful to
future volumes, please send them to us
for possible future publication.
Full photo credits will be given upon
publication.

ISBN 962-361-690-2
printed in Hong Kong

Introduction

This book is a pictorial account of US Army GIs in the European Theater of Operations in Northwest Europe from D-Day, 6 June 1944 to the end of the war in German in May 1945. The special focus of this book is on the infantry in its many forms: regular infantry, paratroopers, the armored doughs of the armored infantry battalions, and Rangers. The emphasis here is on photos of GIs in combat to provide military enthusiasts including modelers, collectors, and re-enactors with a wide variety of photos showing the range of combat uniforms and equipment of US Army infantry during World War II.

The US Army Infantry Division

The US Army infantry division in the ETO in 1944 was generally based on the 15 July 1943 table of organization and equipment. The division was triangular in organization, and its primary components were three infantry regiments. The infantry regiments were supported by a variety of specialized units including the division headquarters, divisional artillery, a mechanized cavalry reconnaissance troop, an engineer battalion, medical battalion, military police platoon, quartermaster company, signal company, and an ordnance light maintenance company. In total, the division had a nominal strength of 13,688 men without attachments such as bands, etc.

It was soon found in combat that the infantry division did not have enough firepower or offensive punch, and so it became the practice to regularly attach a tank battalion, and later a tank destroyer battalion to each division. These were not permanent attachments, and it was not unusual for a single tank battalion to be shifted around between various divisions several times during the course of the war. In addition, other specialized units could be temporarily put under divisional control for missions, especially during offensive operations.

The infantry regiment was the basic fighting organization of the division and had 3,258 men. Like the division itself, it was triangular in organization with three infantry battalions each with 871 men plus supporting sub-units. The infantry regiment had its own organic fire support in the form of a cannon company with six towed 105mm howitzers, and a towed anti-tank company with nine M1 57mm anti-tank guns.

The infantry battalion, like the regiment, was triangular and consisted of three rifle companies. They were lettered in sequence so that the 1st Battalion had Companies A, B, C; 2nd Battalion had D, E, F, etc. Besides the rifle companies, the battalion had a modest amount of fire support in the form of three 57mm anti-tank guns, and six 81mm mortars. The rifle companies were also triangular, with three rifle platoons, each of which had three squads.

The rifle platoon consisted of a headquarters with the platoon leader, platoon sergeant, platoon guide, and two messengers, along with the three rifle squads. The platoon leader was usually a 1st or 2nd lieutenant armed with a M1 carbine, though in combat the M1 Garand rifle was favored. Each rifle squad consisted of twelve men led by a staff sergeant, a "buck" sergeant

assistant squad leader, and ten privates. The men were armed with the M1 Garand rifle except for one who was armed with the squad's automatic weapon, the BAR (Browning Automatic Rifle) though some squads had a "sniper" with the older bolt-action Springfield rifle. The assistant squad leader was nominally the unit's "grenadier" for firing rifle grenades from his M1 rifle, though in fact any of the squad rifles could be fit with a grenade adapter and often were in combat. GIs were notorious for supplementing their firepower once in combat with unauthorized weapons, and it was not uncommon for squads to end up with more than a single BAR, or for rifleman to obtain .45 cal Thompson submachine guns. Each squad was also equipped with a 2.35 inch rocket launcher, better known as the bazooka, for anti-tank defense. This weapon had a mixed reputation. In skilled and brave hands, it was a formidable weapon against tanks when used at close ranges, but its rocket ammunition was temperamental in field conditions, and it was not effective against the thicker German armor, such as the glacis plate of the dreaded Panther tank.

During the opening stages of the fighting in France, most GIs wore the M1941 field jacket in a light khaki shade of olive drab and the M1941 wool trousers, in a brownish shade of olive drab. The newer M1943 battledress gradually began to appear which can be distinguished by the field jacket with its additional breast pockets. The new M1943 battledress was in a greener shade, and was part of a general program to darken the color of Army battledress away from the faded khaki color of the early war years. Although these uniforms prove practical in the summer and fall of 1944, the Army Quartermaster was unprepared for the harsh conditions of the winter of 1944-45. As a result, units received a hodge-podge of winter wear including overcoats, mackinaws, and various types of sweaters intended to provide layers under the M1943 field jacket. The biggest scandal was over winter boots. The US Army did not take adequate steps to prevent trench foot, which became a major cause of casualties in the winter fighting. Steps were taken to more widely distribute shoe-pacs, rubber lined arctic boots and other forms of specialized footwear, but many GIs suffered through November-December 1944 with cold and soggy boots.

Acknowledgements

This books consists entirely of photos taken by the US Army's Signal Corps during World War II. The author collected these photos from a variety of locations, including their original depository in the Pentagon until the late 1970s, then the Defense Audio-Visual Agency at the Anacostia Navy Yard, and finally, the current repository at the US National Archives and Records Administration in College Park, Maryland. Other sources of Signal Corps photos used in this book include the Special Collections at the US Military Academy at West Point, NY, the Military History Institute at the Army War College in Carlisle Barracks, PA, and the Patton Museum at Ft. Knox, KY. The author would like to thank Alan Aimone, of USMA; Randy Hackenburg of MHI; and Charles Lemons and Candace Fuller of the Patton Museum for their help in locating material used in this book.

Prior to the D-Day airborne landings, some of the paratroopers decided to adopt Mohawk haircuts and war-paint as seen here at the staging base in Britain on 5 June 1944. The censor has obscured the Screaming Eagle divisional patch of the 101st Airborne Division.

GIs of the 4th Infantry Division on an LCT assault craft on D-Day prior to their landing at Utah Beach. The landings at Utah were far less costly than those at neighboring Omaha by the 1st and 29th Divisions.

Troops of one of the Engineer Special Brigades come ashore at Normandy on 7 June 1944, identifiable by their helmet markings. These were one of a number of specialized units that were deployed to help secure the beaches.

Besides the army troops at Normandy, the Navy's 6th and 7th Naval Beach Battalions also took part, as well as other specialized units. Here, a Naval Shore Fire Control Party of the JASCO (Joint Assault Signal Company) are seen in operation near Les Dunes de Varredville on 10 June using a SCR-284 with hand-operated generator while the soldier to the right is using a SCR-586 handie-talkie. This is a naval liaison section which was composed of a naval gunfire liaison officer and three radio operators.

Paratroopers patrol through a church ground in Normandy on 8 June 1944. They are readily distinguishable from regular infantry by their M1942 jacket and trousers with the cargo pockets, and the M1C helmet with its distinctive chin restraint.

A pair of GIs enjoy the company of a young French woman in Normandy shortly after the landings. The censor has obscured the divisional patches on their field jackets.

Following the invasion, engineers were kept very busy clearing the beaches and the immediate coastal areas of the thousands of mines that the Germans had laid. This engineer is using the standard SCR-625 mine-detector near the beach on 13 June 1944. The painted insignia on his helmet identifies him as belonging to one of the Engineer Special Brigades.

GIs were often curious about enemy weapons, and here a lieutenant test-fires a German *panzerschreck* anti-tank rocket launcher in a church yard in Normandy on 17 June 1944. This was a more powerful anti-tank weapon than the American bazooka which inspired it.

The infantry division's heavy fire power came from its M1 155mm howitzer like this one being moved forward on 17 June 1944 in Normandy. There were six of these in each of the three infantry regiments and 36 in divisional artillery. The standard prime mover for this weapon was the M5 high speed tractor as seen here.

GIs use a roadside drainage ditch for cover during a skirmish near St. Saveur le Vicomte on 21 June 1944. In the background to the right is their 1½ton weapons carrier while to the left is an abandoned German truck.

The US Army was stymied for much of June and July in the *bocage* country south of the Normandy beaches. These dense hedgerows gave the Germans ideal defensive positions, and necessitated a bloody infantry advance towards St. Lo. This GI from the 29th Division has cut a firing hole through some *bocage* during the fighting on 8 July 1944.

An artilleryman in an infantry cannon company grimaces as he fires his M3 105mm pack howitzer near Carentan on 11 July 1944. Some infantry cannon companies used this light weight 105mm pack howitzer instead of the more common M2A1 105mm howitzer, but its inferior range led the infantry to favor the M2A1. The divisional patch on the gunner's shoulder appears to be that of the 90th Division, whose 357th Infantry fought at Carentan.

A German officer is interrogated by a sergeant from the 35th Division during the intense fighting near St. Lo on 16 July 1944. There was an ample supply of German-speaking GIs due to the sizeable German emigration to the United States in the decades before the war.

A good study of an engineer at work with a SCR-625 mine-detector. The small cylindrical device on his shoulder is an audio alarm which signaled when metal was detected. Mine sweepers usually operated in two-man teams with the other engineer probing for the mine using a bayonet.

After a month of bloody fighting in the *bocage*, the US infantry fought its way to the outskirts of the city of St. Lo, opening up the prospects for a breakout from Normandy. The scenery here on 21 July is fairly typical of the region, with a country road running between two thick hedgerows on either side.

Although not identified, these two GIs are probably scouts from an armored cavalry reconnaissance squadron in the St. Lo area on 21 July 1944. The sergeant to the left is armed with a .45 cal pistol and carries a SCR-528 handie-talkie on his right shoulder while the private to the right is armed with a M1 carbine.

A squad from the 17th Engineer Battalion, 2nd Armored Division move up near Canisy, France on 27 July 1944 during Operation Cobra. They are one of the few units issued the M1942 herringbone twill (HBT) two piece camouflage battledress for Operation Cobra. The camouflage quickly became unpopular as it was often mistaken for German camouflage.

A M2 half-track of the 41st Armored Infantry, 2nd Armored Division moves forward during Operation Cobra. This is one of several half-tracks in the division that had been fitted with a 37mm anti-tank gun taken from obsolete M6 gun motor carriages after the North African campaign. The gun is obscured by the troops around it, and its usual armored shield has been removed. The GIs are wearing the M1942 HBT two-piece camouflage suit.

An armored dough from the 41st Armored Infantry, 2nd Armored Division having a little chow during a lull in the fighting near Pont Brocard. This gives a good view of the M1942 HBT camouflage suit worn by this unit during Operation Cobra. It was largely abandoned after August 1944 due to the confusion it caused with German camouflage uniforms.

A group of officers from the 41st Armored Infantry, 2nd Armored Division discuss their plans at Pont Brocard in July 1944. All are wearing the controversial M1942 HBT two-piece camouflage battledress.

An 81mm mortar team from the 79th Division moves through La Haye de Puits in late July 1944 during Operation Cobra, the breakout from Normandy. The soldier to the immediate left of the road-sign is carrying the heavy mortar base-plate, and the squad is wearing the canvas weight-bearing shoulder pads issued to mortar teams. Behind them, one of the squad is carrying additional ammunition in an M2 ammunition bag which was worn like a life-vest over the head, with pouches on the front and back.

In the wake of the rapid US advance, an engineer mine-clearing team goes to work in the town square of Lessay on 28 July 1944. One engineer operates the SCR-625 mine-detector while the other probes for the mine using a bayonet.

A GI of the 2nd Battalion, 331st Infantry, 83rd Division near Coutances during Operation Cobra on 29 July 1944. He is armed with a M3A1 "Grease Gun" which was not yet in widespread use with infantry units at this stage of the war. At first, it was issued mainly as a self-defense weapon for tank and vehicle crews, later as a substitute for the Thompson sub-machine gun.

A GI walks across an improvised footbridge near St. Germain on 30 July 1944. He is carrying a M1919A4 .30 cal light machine gun on his shoulder, as well as a M1 rifle slung over his shoulder. Machine gunners generally were not armed with rifles but carried a pistol for self-defense due to the weight of the machine gun.

The German response to Operation Cobra was a panzer offensive codenamed *Luttich* aimed at cutting off the lead elements of the US 12th Army Group. The offensive was stopped cold by the stalwart defense of the 30th Infantry Division in and around the town of Mortain. Here, an officer of the 117th Infantry, 30th Division uses a field telephone from his trench near St. Bartholomey. To either side are two SCR-536 "handie-talkie", a small hand-held AM transceiver used at platoon level. They are frequently misidentified as "walkie-talkies" which was in fact the name for the back-pack SCR-300 radio.

An exhausted GI from the 12th Infantry, 4th Infantry Division takes a break near Villedieu on 3 August 1944 during the Normandy fighting. Like many GIs, he kept papers and letters inside the helmet lining to keep them dry.

A .30 cal M1917A1 light machine gun team cover a street corner in Angers in the Loire valley during the drive of Patton's Third Army toward the Seine. The city was taken on 10-11 August by the 5th Infantry Division.

The most intense fighting in the Brittany peninsula took place around the ports, especially St. Malo and Brest. Here a .30 cal. M1917A1 machine gun team from the 331st Infantry, 83rd Division take up positions on a street in the town. St. Malo proved an especially difficult objective due to the thick fortified walls around the town and its many waterways.

GIs from the 331st Infantry slowly advance through St. Malo on 8 August 1944. The 83rd Division began its assault on the Breton port on 7 August, and the final German hold-outs in the old citadel did not surrender until 17 August.

Although overshadowed by the airborne landings in Normandy, the amphibious invasion of southern France by the Seventh US Army on 15 August 1944 had its own airborne landing. Here, troops of the 1st Airborne Task Force disembark from their CG-4A gliders after the landings near Le Motte as part of Operation Dragoon.

A 60mm mortar team in action near Perriers en Beaufice on 12 August 1944. The solider to the right is equipped with a SCR-586 handie-talkie, a small hand-held radio transmitter-receiver originally designed for paratrooper use. The US Army was the only force in World War II to widely use radios such as this at platoon level.

A squad of GIs do house-to-house searches in an unidentified French town during the fighting on the approaches to Paris on 15 August 1944. They are all armed with the standard M1 Garand rifle except the second GI from the left who is carrying a BAR squad automatic weapon.

Leading the charge into Brittany was the 6th Armored Division. Here, a group of officers and NCOs from one of the division's armored infantry battalions discuss plans while in Armamre, France on 17 August 1944.

One of the first rules of the infantry is to rest when you can. GIs of the 3rd Infantry Division take a break near Brignoles, France on 18 August 1944, three days after the start of the southern France landings. This division had previously been involved in the fighting in the Anzio beach-head in Italy before being committed to the fighting in southern France.

13

Patton's Third Army raced into Brittany after Operation Cobra but were stymied by the heavy defenses of the seacoast towns. Here, a GI armed with a Thompson submachine gun takes cover behind a hedge during the fighting on the outskirts of Brest on 26 August 1944.

A cavalryman of the 87th Cavalry Recon Squadron (Mecz) of the 7th Armored Division fires on German positions during fighting near Epernay on 27 August 1944. When fighting dismounted, the cavalry used the M1 .30 cal carbine rather than the M1 .30 cal Garand rifle used by the infantry.

Heavy artillery was brought in to shell the German defenses at Brest, leading to a lunar landscape in some sectors, like in this area being held by the 23rd Infantry, 2nd Infantry Division on 29 August 1944.

GIs cautiously advance into Brest during the fighting there on 9 September 1944. The city finally fell after a concerted infantry assault on 19 September 1944.

A M1 57mm anti-tank gun defends a corner in the shattered port city of Brest during the fighting in September 1944. The 57mm anti-tank gun was the standard anti-tank weapon of the infantry divisions, and was a license copy of the British 6 pdr. The sign behind the gun is for a local clothing store.

An armored dough of an armored infantry battalion of the 7th Armored Division finds a French helmet near an old trench line from World War I in the Argonne forest on 31 August 1944. He is armed with a Thompson .45 cal submachine gun. In contrast to regular infantry, the .45 cal submachine gun was authorized equipment for the armored doughs.

A group of infantrymen sit around a record player for a bit of entertainment during a lull in the fighting at the seaport of Brest on 11 September 1944. The GI to the immediate left of the record player is wearing the M1942 HBT camouflage suit, a battledress that was beginning to disappear by this time.

GIs of the 80th Division use a rubber assault raft to cross the Meuse river near St. Mihiel on 1 September 1944. The town was the site of famous US Army battle in World War I.

GIs from the 358th Infantry, 90th Division take shelter in a trench leading into an old German bunker with the inscription "Viel feind, viel Her" (Many enemies, Much Honor) on 12 September 1944 during the Lorraine campaign. The 90th Division had the reputation as being the worst US division in Normandy, but after a change of leadership in the late summer, became one of the best. A few days before the division had decimated Panzer Brigade 106, led by the legendary panzer commander Franz Bake, in a confused night battle near the village of Mairy.

While Hodge's First US Army was advancing through Belgium, Patton's Third US Army was advancing through the Lorraine region to the south with its eye on the Saar. GIs from the 5th Infantry Division move assault boats forward to the Moselle river on 8 September 1944 as part of Patton's attempt to breach the German defenses along this formidable river barrier. The DIVISION created a shallow bridgehead over the river at Dornot but it was bombarded from Fort St. Blaise, part of the Metz fortification line, and had to be withdrawn several days later.

GIs use a ladder to scale a small fence during the fighting around Mirecourt, France on 14 September 1944 during Patton's attacks in Lorraine. The GI to the left is wearing the pre-war M1928 haversack, still a common item in the summer and fall of 1944.

Patton's dream of a quick advance into the Saar were frustrated in the fall of 1944 when the Allied armies' logistics became overextended. Failing to capture the fortress city of Metz on the run during the Lorraine campaign, his infantry divisions began a series of frustrating attacks on the outer fortifications. These two riflemen wait by a roadside in the outskirts of Metz during the fighting there in October 1944.

Following the lightning advance through France in August, the First US Army raced through Belgium in early September on its way to the German frontier. Here, a machine-gunner of the 5th Infantry Division is seen carrying a M1917A1 water-cooled .30 cal Browning light machine gun. For personal defense, he is armed with the M3 .45 cal "grease gun".

GIs congregate around a German prisoner wounded during the fighting in Ramillies, Belgium on 6 September 1944, Two of the GIs are armed with .45 cal Thompson submachine guns while the rifleman in the center is armed with a BAR.

GIs advance warily through Thimaster, Belgium on 11 September 1944. Various German military road-signs can be seen scrawled on the door and walls. Their armament, a pair of M1 carbines and a Thompson sub-machine gun suggest they may be from an armored cavalry reconnaissance squadron.

A machine gun team of the 8th Infantry, 4th Infantry Division man a Browning M1917A1 .30 cal light machine gun while a M4 medium tank of the 70th Tank Battalion probes forward near Roth, Germany on 15 September 1944 during the initial fighting on the German frontier. By the end of the day, the regiment had pushed to the edge of the Siegfried line defenses. The Siegfried line was also called the Westwall by the Germans.

GIs of the 39th Infantry, 9th Infantry Division advance through German concrete road obstructions during their advance through the Siegfried line on 15 September 1944. The hasty German retreat of August-September 1944 left sections of the Siegfried line lightly defended, but once the German defenses coalesced later in the month, the attacks on the Westwall defense proved much more difficult.

Paratroopers of the 82nd Airborne Division prepare for Operation Market-Garden at the airbase at Cottesmore on 17 September 1944 with their C-47 transport aircraft behind them. This airborne operation was planned to provide the Allies with quick access to the east bank of the Rhine through the Netherlands, but the failure to seize the final bridge at Arnhem doomed the operation.

Paratroopers of the 82nd Airborne Division advance along a road in Holland on 18 September 1944 during Operation Market Garden. Although its bumper codes are partially obscured, the jeep appears to belong to the division's 307th Airborne Engineer Battalion which was landed by glider.

Dutch children welcome paratroopers of the 101st Airborne Division on 18 September 1944 during Operation Market-Garden. The paratroopers had been largely refitted with the M1943 battledress after Normandy, modified with cargo pockets on the trousers.

Glider infantry of the 101st Airborne Division congregate around a smashed Waco CG-4A glider in the Netherlands during Operation Market-Garden on 18 September 1944. The objectives of the two US airborne divisions during the operation were key bridges on the approach to the Rhine bridge at Arnhem which they managed to seize in conjunction with British armored units.

An engineer of the 133rd Engineer Battalion mans a M1917A1 .30 cal water-cooled light machine gun on the approaches to a Bailey bridge being constructed on the Seille river near Bioncourt, France on 6 October 1944. By this stage, this region of Lorraine was in the rear areas of the front and the bridge was being constructed to improve logistics northeast of the city of Nancy.

A M5 3-inch anti-tank gun provides support to the 117th Infantry, 30th Division during the fighting in Schauffenburg, Germany on 9 October, along with a bazooka team and a .50 cal heavy machine gun. The day before, Kampfgruppe von Fritzchen from Panzer Brigade 108 had attacked the regiment with eleven tanks and twenty-three StuG-III assault guns and was finally beaten off with help from M4 tanks of the 743rd Tank Battalion. The 3-inch anti-tank gun was not organic to infantry division, and was used only by special towed tank destroyer battalions which were attached to infantry divisions for specific operations.

While Bradley's 12th Army Group was assaulting the Siegfried line through Belgium, Dever's 6th Army Group was advancing to the south through the Vosges region of France. A radioman from the 36th Division is seen here with the standard SCR-300 radio in the town of Vagney on 17 October 1944. He is wearing the much prized winter combat jacket, usually issued to armored vehicle crews but sometimes seen in infantry units. At company level, the US infantry used the man-pack SCR-300 "walkie-talkie" FM transceiver to communicate with the battalion and higher headquarters.

A M1919A4 .30 cal light machine team is seen here in action in Aachen on 15 October 1944. Aachen was the first German city assaulted by the US Army and after having reached the outskirts in September, the final assault into the city began on 11 October.

A M1 57mm anti-tank gun takes part in the fighting in Aachen on 16 October 1944. Although intended for defense against tanks, the infantry regiments frequently used the gun to provide direct fire support using high explosive ammunition.

A rifleman of the 110th Infantry, 28th Division during fighting near Kohlscheid on 17 October 1944 during the fighting for the Siegfried line. This division was raised from the Pennsylvania National Guard.

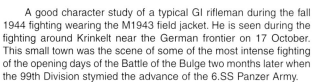

A good character study of a typical GI rifleman during the fall 1944 fighting wearing the M1943 field jacket. He is seen during the fighting around Krinkelt near the German frontier on 17 October. This small town was the scene of some of the most intense fighting of the opening days of the Battle of the Bulge two months later when the 99th Division stymied the advance of the 6.SS Panzer Army.

A scout jeep of the 442nd Infantry (Nisei-Separate) on patrol near Chambois on 13 October 1944. This regiment was formed from Japanese-American volunteers, and had begun its attack on Bruyeres.

The workhorse of the infantry's artillery battalions was the M2A1 105mm howitzer, seen here in action near Bruyeres, France on 18 October 1944 with the 442nd Infantry (Nisei-Separate). Each infantry regiment had six 105mm howitzers.

A trio of tired GIs from the 79th Division in Laneuville, France on 25 October 1944 following the fighting for the high ground east of Embermenil. The division had been relieved the day before after months of hard fighting in Lorraine, and was sent to Luneville for recuperation.

A couple of engineers of the 167th Engineer Battalion, attached to the 6th Armored Division, conduct mine clearing on a road near Luppy, France on 15 November 1944. The GI in the center in the winter makinaw is operating a SCR-625 mine detector with the associated electronics in the pack strapped behind him. He is wearing the small audio warning buzzer on his chest. The GI to the left in the greatcoat is carrying a bayonet to probe for the mine once it is found.

U.S. Tank Crew, Northwest Europe

Beyond the standard GI uniform that every tank crewman was entitled to wear, certain items are generally associated with armored combat dress. Most obvious was the M1942 armored forces helmet. It was designed as a means of protecting the user from the many dangerous protrusions within a lurching tank. Further, it provided a means of supporting communications headphones. The dome of the helmet and the nape protector were made from compressed cardboard composite material and the remainder was made of leather. A removable headphone was fitted into each ear flap while the throat microphone was a separate item. The M1 steel helmet, without its liner, could be worn directly over the tanker's helmet, providing ballistic protection when necessary.

The winter combat jacket was primarily issued to armored troops but it was much coveted by others. The wind and waterproof garment was lined with blanket material and had knit cuffs and collar. In warmer months, it was worn with the issue wool trousers or over one-piece HBT coveralls. During colder months, blanket lined winter combat trousers could be worn. These were a bib type of overall with a zipper front opening and zipper

openings at the sides that allowed access to trouser pockets beneath. A relief zipper was also provided. Earlier variants were more simply constructed. The winter combat helmet was a close fitting cloth hood that provided similar warmth as the winter jacket and trousers. It could be worn beneath the fiber tanker's helmet.

A variety of goggles were issued including M1944 Polaroid and M1938 Resistol types. Web equipment was generally limited to the M1936 pistol belt with a M1911A1 pistol in the M1916 leather holster. An ammo pouch and first aid pouch were generally in evidence on the belt. Occasionally the pistol was carried in the M3 shoulder holster instead.

Unit insignia was commonly worn on the left shoulder of the jacket and rank chevrons could be seen on both arms.

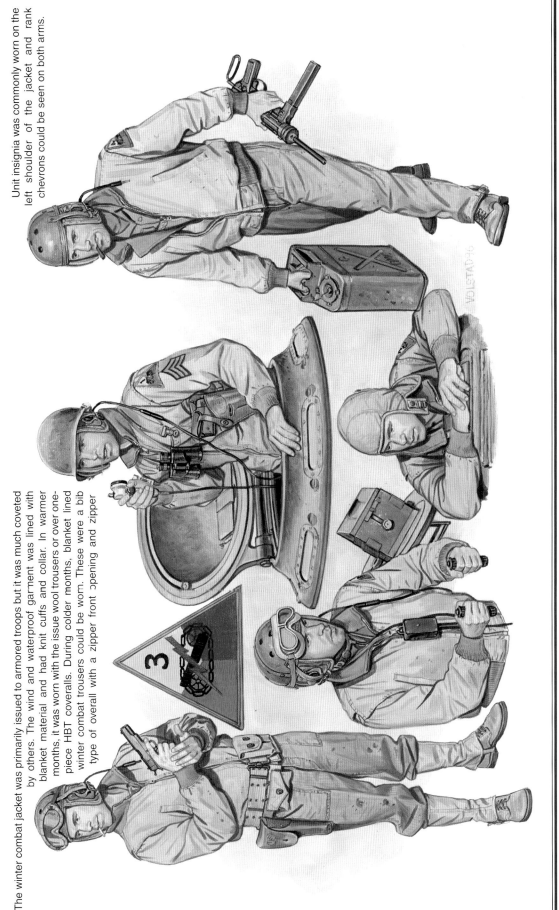

Private, 4th Infantry Division, France 1944

The herringbone twill work uniform was commonly worn as a field uniform in 1944. On D-Day, some units had HBT's that had been impregnated against chemical weapons and wore these over the wool uniform. The most common version of HBT jacket had a pair of large expandable chest pockets while the trousers had similar cargo pockets below the waist on each side. While some of the 4th Division did wear their unit patch, it wasn't particularly common to see any insignia worn on HBT's.

The rifleman's web-gear is centered on his M1923 cartridge belt. On it, he carries an M1942 first aid pouch and an M1910 canteen. His M1 bayonet and M1910 entrenching tool are attached to the M1928 haversack. Both items could be hooked on his cartridge belt should the need arise. Extra ammunition for his M1 Garand was carried in cloth bandoleers slung across the body. Often a knot was tied in the strap of the bandoleer to shorten it and prevent it from swinging. Slung across the other shoulder is a multi-purpose ammunition bag. It could contain grenades or any combination of items.

The M1 helmet has a camouflage net attached. The excess netting was simply held between the liner and the outer shell. There were a number of different nets used with varying mesh openings. The chinstrap was often fastened over the rear rim of the helmet as it was believed that the concussion from a near miss could case a neck injury if a helmet was fastened securely. Not all subscribed to that theory.

VOLSTAD '02

First Lieutenant, 9th Infantry Division, France 1944

This young officer wears the uniform that is perhaps most associated with the US Army soldier in WWII. Basically, it consisted of the winter service wool shirt and trousers and it was not uncommon for officers to wear the enlisted rank's uniform items in the field. The M1941 Field Jacket olive drab (OD) was standard throughout the war although the M1943 Combat Field Jacket had largely replaced it by the end of action in 1945.

The service shoe, worn with M1938 leggings, dismounted pattern also remained in use until war's end. Initially the leggings were 13 inches tall with 9 hooks but were shortened to 12 inches with 8 hooks. The service shoe was initially smooth russet leather with toecaps but in 1943, new ankle boots were issued with the rough side out. If properly greased, these boots provided superior weatherproofing.

It was standard practice for officers to display their rank on the front of their M1 helmet. Additionally, in some circumstances, a vertical white stripe was painted on the back of the helmet to identify that the wearer was an officer to those following. NCO's would display a similar horizontal stripe for the same purpose.

His web gear includes a M1936 pistol belt supported by M1936 suspenders. On the belt are carried an M1911A1 pistol in a russet leather holster, ammunition pouches for it and his M1 carbine, M1942 first aid pouch, M17 case for M3 binoculars, M1910 canteen and M1943 entrenching tool. It would be probable that an M3 fighting knife would have been carried as well. Hooked on his suspender is a TL122C angle-head flashlight. Completing his gear is an M1938 dispatch case.

101st Airborne Division, Belgium 1944

With the realization that the German offensive in the Ardennes was a serious threat, the 101st Airborne Division was rushed into the line near Bastogne. By the winter of 1944, US paratroopers wore little that was unique to the Airborne. Those that still had them would wear their jump boots but the M1943 double buckle combat service shoe was just as likely to be seen.

The M1943 jacket and trousers were worn instead of the light OD M1942 uniform (a change that was made for Operation Market-Garden in September). Cargo pockets were rigged to the sides of the trousers but it would seem that not all members of the 101st had the modified trousers when they shipped out to Bastogne. In fact they were short of almost all the necessities from winter clothing to weapons and much of it was acquired after they went into action.

While the M1942 overcoat remained the standard source of warmth, it was a cumbersome garment that became heavier as it soaked up moisture. Identical to the 1939 pattern, it differed in having buttons of OD plastic rather than brass. The hip-length Mackinaw was perhaps a reasonable

alternative to the overcoat but it doesn't seem to have been nearly as common in the field. There were three distinct variations of this "jeep coat" (as it came to be known), mainly related to the collar design. While there were no doubt exceptions, insignia seldom seems to appear on these heavy outer garments.

For the most part, it is difficult to tell if the helmets worn by US Airborne troops were the M1 or M1C. With the chin cup of the M1C removed and its "A" frame tucked up inside, only the web chinstrap and its "D" shaped bales are left to make the identification. While many helmets worn by the 101st in the Ardennes still bore the unit markings on the side, many were unmarked and helmet nets were often absent.

Whatever the footwear being worn, overshoes were gratefully accepted as they kept the feet dry and provided some insulation. The Arctic Overshoes were initially all rubber items but to conserve resources, the uppers were then made from canvas. Later issue were again made totally from rubber. The leather and rubber shoepac doesn't seem to have been available in NW Europe until January 1945, well after the Ardennes Offensive had been defeated.

An infantry trench line in an unidentified woods in the German border area on 4 November 1944. In the center of the photo is a water-cooled M1917A1 .30 cal Browning machine gun. The area between the Belgian border and the Roer river was heavily wooded and would be the scene of the savage Hurtgen forest fighting two weeks later.

Flamethrowers were not widely used by the US Army in France, but were issued in greater numbers once the fortifications of the Siegfried line were encountered in September 1944. This flamethrower team from the 30th Division is practicing with a man-portable flamethrower near Aachen, Germany on 5 November 1944.

GIs from the 398th Infantry, 100th Division move through the woods near Raon l'Etape during the fighting in the High Vosges mountains on 17 November 1944. Most of the troops are wearing the M1943 field jacket and trousers.

Medics attend to a wounded GI from the 8th Infantry, 4th Infantry Division during fighting around Duren, Germany on 18 November 1944 shortly after the start of the fighting in the Hurtgen forest. This was one of the bloodiest infantry battles fought by the US Army in World War II.

A group of GIs of the 398th Infantry, 100th Division move through the woods near Bitche, France on 18 December 1944 during the fighting for Fort Schiesseck, part of the Maginot line of border forts. These soldiers form a .30 cal machine gun team with the soldier to the left carrying ammunition, the soldier in the center carrying the .30 cal machine gun and the soldier in the background carrying the tripod. There were six of these machine guns in each infantry battalion, two per company.

A rifleman of the 104th Division prepares to fire a rifle grenade from his M1 Garand rifle during the fighting for Stolberg on 16 November 1944. To fire rifle grenades from the Garand, the rifleman had to attach a small extension to the gun barrel on which the grenade was mounted. The 104th Division had relieved the 1st "Big Red One" Division in the fight for Stolberg on 8-10 November.

GIs man a defensive position on the outskirts of the Hurtgen forest at the start of the bloody battle there on 17 November 1944. The M1 57mm anti-tank gun was the standard anti-tank gun in infantry divisions in 1944, with eighteen in each infantry regiment. Although largely ineffective against heavier German tanks like the Panther and Tiger, it still had bite when attacking them from the flank.

A GI of the 29th Division armed with a bazooka races past a Jagdpanzer 38(t) assault gun he has knocked out during the fighting near Aldenhoven, Germany on 21 November 1944.

Pvt. Robert Starkey of the 16th Infantry, 1st Infantry Division stands beside the burnt-out hulk of a Jagdpanzer IV tank destroyer he knocked out with his bazooka near Hamich, Germany on 22 November 1944. The bazooka explosion detonated the vehicle's ammunition, leading to a catastrophic internal fire which blew open the vehicle superstructure.

A rifleman from Company G, 335th Infantry, 84th Division during the fighting near Beeck, Germany on 29 November 1944 during the start of the division's attack towards the Roer river. He is wearing the older M1928 haversack and the standard M1943 combat boots.

Because US tanks used FM radios and the infantry used AM radios, communication during joint operations below battalion level could be tricky. In the summer of 1944, Ordnance units began installing telephones mounted in .30 cal ammunition boxes, to the rear of the M4 medium tanks and hooked into the tank intercom system. This allowed the infantry to communicate with the tank when it was buttoned up. This is an example of a GI from the 81st Division using the tank phone on a M4 medium tank from the 709th Tank Battalion during fighting for Zweifall, Germany on 24 November 1944.

A GI from the 313th Infantry, 79th Division rounds up prisoners after the fighting in Oberhoffen in the Alsace region of France on 8 December 1944. He is wearing the M1943 field jacket with the attached hood. The 79th Division fought for Hagenau over the next four days during the Seventh US Army's drive to push beyond Alsace into Germany.

An 81mm mortar team from the 2nd Battalion, 22nd Infantry, 4th Infantry Division fires in support of its regiment, locked in fighting in the woods near Grosshau, Germany on 1 December 1944. The woods around this town were the scene of some of the fiercest fighting of the battle for the Hurtgen forest, and in the first two weeks of fighting this regiment suffered 86 percent casualties, and 140 percent casualties by the end of the fighting later in December.

GIs of the 109th Infantry, 103rd Division enter Keffenaach, France on 14 December during the fighting along the German frontier. The unit crossed the Lauter river into Germany the following day after two weeks of fighting. The troops are wearing the M1943 field jacket with the hood attached.

A pair of GIs wearing makinaws rest under the cover of a M4 medium tank during the fighting near Gleich, Germany on 11 December 1944. The .30 cal ammunition box evident above the head of the soldier on the right contains a telephone hooked into the tank's intercom system, allowing the infantry to communicate with the crew in combat when the tank is buttoned up.

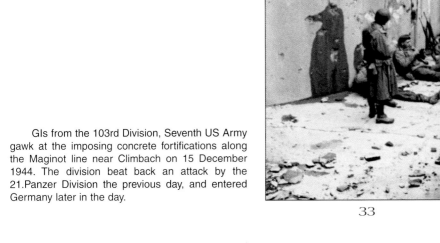

GIs from the 103rd Division, Seventh US Army gawk at the imposing concrete fortifications along the Maginot line near Climbach on 15 December 1944. The division beat back an attack by the 21.Panzer Division the previous day, and entered Germany later in the day.

33

A patrol from the 3rd Battalion, 180th Infantry, 45th Division warily approach a house in Bobenthal, Germany on 16 December 1944 during the fighting along the upper reaches of the Lauter river. The GI to the left is armed with a Thompson sub-machine gun.

An officer from the 83rd Division brings in a haul of German automatic weapons after the unit had repulsed a heavy German attack near Durn and Guerzenich during the Roer fighting on 16 December 1944. He is carrying a pair of MP-40 "burp guns" on this right arm, and a pair of MG-42 machine guns in his left hand. These were not commonly used by US troops due to the ammunition problem and the fact that their distinctive sound could lead to problems with neighboring units. In the background is a M20 armored utility car.

A GI from the 115th Infantry, 29th Division fires some captured German 8cm ammunition from his M1 81mm mortar during defensive operations near Pier, Germany on 15 January 1945. The German ammunition case can be seen to the left. The ammunition was compatible between the German and American mortar as they were both derived from the French Stokes-Brandt mortar. Each US infantry battalion had six of these mortars.

During the fighting in the Ardennes, some of the sectors along the Siegfried line remained quiet until January 1945. The 79th Division reached Scheibenhardt in mid-December, and as seen from this 314th Infantry dugout on 2 January 1945, remained on the defensive for two weeks. The GIs have added a heater to the dugout, and the GI on sentry duty has his M1 rifle propped up on two branches, and a beer stein handy for refreshment.

One of the classic images from the Battle of the Bulge as two armored doughs from the 4th Armored Division take aim at targets in the field outside Bastogne on 27 December 1944. The 4th Armored Division was the first unit from Patton's Third Army to break into Bastogne, and assisted in the push towards Houfallize to cut off the German bulge. The rifleman in the foreground is wearing the winter combat jacket issued to armored vehicle crewmen, and often worn in the armored infantry battalions as well.

A chaplain talks with a platoon from the 504th Parachute Infantry Regiment, 82nd Airborne Division near Cheneux, Belgium on 28 December 1944. This legendary paratroop unit began its counter-attacks against the German forces the day before. While the battledress of the airborne troops in the Battle of the Bulge differed little from other GIs, some distinctive features are evident such as the extra cargo pockets on the trousers of the GI in the center of the photo.

A trio of GIs in Malmédy on 29 December 1944 show the typical mixture of winter dress during the Ardennes fighting. The GIs on the right and left are wearing the wool overcoat while the GI in the center is wearing the M1943 field jacket layered with sweaters underneath. The two GIs to the right are wearing the rubber coated cloth-top arctic overshoes.

An armored dough of the 36th Armored Infantry, 3rd Armored Division mans a M1919A4 .30 cal Browning light machine gun in a wooded area along the roads leading to Liege, Belgium, the German objective during the Ardennes offensive. Behind him is one of the division's M4 medium tanks. This division along with the 2nd Armored Division were rushed into the Ardennes before Christmas and blunted the armored spearheads of the Fifth Panzer Army in a series of violent engagements near Manhay, Grandmenil, and Celles.

An engineer from the 3rd Armored Division emplaces a M1A1 anti-tank mine in a road near Hotton during the fighting on 28 December 1944. There was intense tank fighting in this area in the days after Christmas.

A litter team from the 335th Infantry, 84th Division evacuate wounded GIs on stretchers near Amonines, Belgium on 4 January 1945. The division took part in the fighting for Concy over the next few days in conjunction with a combat command from the 2nd Armored Division.

A machine gun team of the 325th Glider Infantry Regiment, 82nd Airborne Division hold defensive positions near Odrimont, Belgium on 6 January 1945. They are armed with a tripod-mounted M1919A4 .30 cal light machine gun which has been fitted with the bipod from a M1919A6 machine gun.

A company of paratroopers from the 82nd Airborne Division wait in reserve during the fighting for Comte on 6 January 1945. They are wearing a typical hodge-podge of winter gear including overcoats and M1943 field jackets and are nearly indistinguishable from any other infantry unit of the time.

Riflemen of the 290th Infantry, 75th Division take up firing positions on the roof of a farm building near Bette, Belgium on 7 January 1945 near the Aisne river. The Ardennes campaign was the division's baptism of fire.

The lack of adequate snow camouflage battledress led to various improvisations. Pvt. Earl Pierce, from an unidentified intelligence and reconnaissance (I&R) platoon, used white paint over his M1943 field dress as seen here on 8 January 1945.

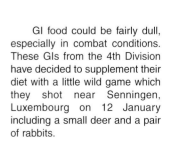

GI food could be fairly dull, especially in combat conditions. These GIs from the 4th Division have decided to supplement their diet with a little wild game which they shot near Senningen, Luxembourg on 12 January including a small deer and a pair of rabbits.

A ski patrol from the 60th Infantry, 9th Infantry Division receive training on 12 January 1945. The troops are wearing improvised snow suits, probably made from bed sheets. The division held defensive position near the Elsenborn ridge during most of the Battle of the Bulge.

A jeep from the 63rd Armored Infantry Battalion, 11th Armored Division brings in a pair of German prisoners near Longchamps, Belgium on 13 January 1945. Typical of scout jeeps, it is armed with a .30 cal light machine gun on a pintle mount.

GIs from the 3rd Battalion, 347th Infantry, 87th Division get a little hot chow during operations in the woods outside La Roche, Belgium on 13 January 1945, the day on which the division made contact with British forces along the Ourthe river. The GIs are wearing overcoats and M1943 field jackets and a few are wearing the improved snowpac boots.

A patrol from the 17th Airborne Division escorts German prisoners taken during the fighting along the Ourthe river on 15 January 1945. The Ardennes was the baptism of fire for the division which was moved into Belgium on Christmas to take part in the counter-offensive against the Germans. The GI to the right is an NCO as is evident from the horizontal bar painted on the back of his helmet, while the medic is an officer based on the vertical bar on his helmet. Airborne forces by this stage of the war generally wore a battledress essentially similar to other infantry units, but with some modifications such as the extra pockets on the M1943 trousers.

GIs from the 84th Division dig in after a skirmish along a tree line near Berismenil on 13 January which left the GI in the foreground dead. The division was taking part in the push to close off the German salient and advanced as far as Grande Morment the next day, before halting to recuperate for a few days after weeks of hard fighting in the Ardennes.

GIs talk to a captured German medic in Rutenbach, Belgium on 24 January 1945. They are apparently suspicious about his medical kit which he has created from a 7.62mm machine gun ammunition box.

A company of the 2nd Battalion, 16th Infantry, 1st Infantry Division advance down a road near Faymonville, Belgium on 18 January 1945. The GIs are wearing improvised snow suits made from white bed-sheets.

Scouts from the 87th Division move forward at the outskirts of Malsheid, Belgium on 29 January 1945. By the end of the Battle of the Bulge, the US Army had contracted with Dutch and Belgian firms to make white snow coveralls, like those seen here, due to a lack of adequate snow camouflage battledress in the supply chain.

A good character study of an "armored dough" sergeant of one of the armored infantry battalions of the 6th Armored Division during the fighting in Luxembourg on 14 February 1945 at the tail end of the Battle of the Bulge. He is wearing an early pattern makinaw with the wool lining on the collar; the later styles lacked the wool facing. He is also wearing a winter combat helmet under his steel helmet, an insulated cloth headgear designed to fit under the tanker's helmet for cold weather insulation, and seen more commonly in armored units than in regular infantry units. He is also wearing the winter-issue shoepacs which gave better protection in wet weather due to the rubber covering of the lower part of the boot.

In the wake of the Battle of the Bulge, the Wehrmacht staged a smaller offensive, Operation Nordwind in the Alsace region of eastern France. Here an armored dough radioman looks on while a M4 medium tank of the 25th Tank Battalion, 14th Armored Division attacks targets in Oberhoffen on 6 February 1945.

Another view of some armored doughs of the 6th Armored Division during operations along the Our River in Luxembourg on 14 February 1945. The GI to the right with the face bandage is wearing winter combat trousers, a type of trouser with bib front usually issued to armored vehicle crews for cold weather. The armored infantry battalions in armored divisions were more apt to end up with items of battledress originally intended for armored vehicle crews compared to the regular infantry divisions.

The light-weight 75mm M1A1 pack howitzer was used primarily in light divisions such as the airborne divisions in place of the 105mm howitzer. This is a howitzer of the cannon company of the 463rd Parachute Field Artillery Battalion supporting the 1st Airborne Tank Force near Hagenau on 29 January 1945 during the repulse of Operation Nordwind. This unit served as the provisional airborne division for the Seventh Army in Alsace.

A medic and another GI of the 70th Division duck for cover during fighting around Behrnem, France on 17 February 1945 during the counter-attacks towards Saarbrueken. The division fought its way through the Siegfried line in early March 1945.

A machine gun team from 63rd Division races forward near Saarguemines, France on 9 February 1945. The machine gunner in the foreground is armed with the M1919A6 light machine gun, a version of the normal M1919A4 light machine gun but fitted with a stock and bipod that was intended to be more mobile than the basic model while offering more firepower than the lighter BAR.

A BAR rifleman from the 253rd Infantry, 63rd Division adjusts his footgear while on watch near Saareguemines, France on 25 January 1945. He is wearing the new snowpac winter boots, and is putting an improvised cloth liner over them for better insulation. Although the snowpacs offered better protection in wet weather, the rubber lower portions were not comfortable in the intense cold.

GIs of the 314th Infantry, 79th Division accept a drink from a woman in one of the border towns between Alsace and Germany on 6 January 1945. The division at the time was involved in combat near Drusenheim along the Moder river.

Troops of the 2nd Infantry Division march through the ruins of Harpenscheid, Germany on 3 February 1945 two days after starting an offensive against the Roer dams. The division had been on the verge of launching similar attacks on 16 December when the German Ardennes offensive struck, and so took part in the defense of the northern shoulder along the Elsenborn ridge instead. Several of the GIs here wear improvised winter camouflage covers on their helmets.

A 57mm anti-tank gun of the 345th Infantry, 87th Division takes up defensive positions near Schonberg, on 4 February 1945 next to a religious grotto. The division assaulted the West Wall from Belgium on 29 January 1945 and began crossing into Germany over the next few days.

A group of GIs carrying captured German weapons walk over to a training area near Gurzenich, Germany on 7 February 1945 to conduct familiarization training with neighboring infantry units prior to Operation Grenade. The solider in the center is armed with a German Sturmgewehr 44 assault rifle while the GI on the right is armed with a German MG-42 7.62mm machine gun.

After its legendary defense of the towns in front of the Elsenborn ridge during the Battle of the Bulge, the 99th Division was later committed to the fighting along the Siegfried line in early February 1945. Here, a GI from the division looks at an armored cupola from a German fortification captured near Hollerath, Germany on 8 February 1945.

A forward machine gun position of the 359th Infantry, 90th Infantry Division armed with a .30 cal M1917A1 water-cooled Browning light machine gun fires on German troops near Habscheid, Germany on 8 February 1945. The division had penetrated through the Siegfried line near the town the day before.

GIs of the 94th Division hug the ground in a muddy ditch during fighting near Sinz, Germany on 7 February 1945 with the 11.Panzer Division. The determined attacks by the 94th Division led the German divisional commander to complain that his division was being needlessly bled to death in operations for which it was ill-suited. That day, the 256th Volksgrenadier Division began to take up the fight against the GIs in the area.

GIs of the 358th Infantry, 90th Division pour through a gap in the dragon's teeth along the Siegfried line on 12 February 1945. The division was heavily engaged in the fighting along the Westwall for most of February 1945. The German concrete roadblock was fitted with steel beams to prevent the passage of tanks, and the beams can be seen lying by the road to the left after they had been removed by US troops.

A heavy machine gun team from the 26th Division pass through the ruins of Saalautern, Germany on 15 February 1945. Following the Battle of the Bulge, the division seized Saarlautern and remained in defensive positions there until late March. There were six of these .50 cal heavy machine guns in each infantry battalion.

A pair of GIs from the 9th Infantry Division demonstrate the difference between the new M9 bazooka and the older M1A1 bazooka during operations near Walseiffen, Germany on 16 February 1945 during renewed fighting in the Huertgen forest. The newer M9 bazooka could be disassembled into two parts to make it easier to carry. Both men are veterans of the division, and wear overseas service stripes above the cuff on the left arm, each indicating six months of service overseas. This division had seen service since the North African landings.

A GI from the 76th Division looks at the damage inflicted on a German armored cupola on 16 February 1945, part of a fortification complex of the Siegfried line overlooking the Sauer river. The division broke through the Siegfried line two days before.

A patrol from the 35th Division prepare to set out on patrol near Arhoven along the Roer river on 17 February 1945. Three of the four GIs in this group were killed in the ensuing action. Three are wearing the M1943 field jacket, which had become common by this stage of the war.

A medic from the 9th Armored Infantry Battalion, 6th Armored Division has chow from the mess tin on his lap during fighting along the Our river on 18 February 1945 prior to the renewed offensive against the Siegfried line two days later. His clothing is typical of winter 1944 battledress for armored doughs including the bib-front winter combat trousers and cloth winter combat helmet, worn under his steel helmet, an item commonly found in armored units.

A group of GIs from the 94th Division fire on German positions near Oberlenken, Germany on 19 February 1945 using a captured MG-42 machine gun. The division had been fighting along the Siegfried line since mid-January and on 19 February breached the Westwall near the Berg-Munzigen autobahn.

A squad of GIs from the 137th Infantry, 35th Division prepare to set out on a scouting patrol near Aphoven, Germany, a few days before the start of Operation Grenade. The soldier kneeling to the left is armed with the squad automatic weapon, a .30 cal BAR, while the solider kneeling in the center has a rifle grenade launcher fitted to the muzzle of his M1 rifle. This division was formed from units of the Nebraska National Guard.

Cavalry scouts of the 6th Cavalry Reconnaissance Squadron use a rubber raft to conduct a reconnaissance patrol near Stolzenbourg, Luxembourg on 20 February 1945. Note that most of the GIs are armed with the M1 carbine, standard in cavalry squadrons, instead of the usual M1 rifle found in infantry units. The troops wear a mixture of M1943 field jackets and the popular winter combat jacket issued to armored troops.

GIs of the 84th Division, part of XIII Corps, move up engineer assault boats to cross the Roer river on 23 February 1945 at the start of Operation Grenade. The first wave of the division's 334th Infantry used the boats to cross, after which the engineers built foot-bridges, and then a treadway bridge.

GIs from an infantry unit of the Ninth Army take up positions in a trench line during Operation Grenade on 23 February 1945 after they have crossed the Roer river. The trench line is littered with inflated waist life-vests that the GIs wore during the crossing. In the center of the position is a M9 bazooka.

GIs of the 29th Division get ready to start an attack over the Roer river near Julich on 23 February 1945. The division had captured parts of the town on the bank of the river after heavy fighting in early December 1944, and captured the rest of the city including its citadel the following day on 24 February 1945 with the help of flame-throwing tanks as part of Operation Grenade.

A squad of GIs of the 84th Division carefully move forward near the Rurich train station on 23 February 1944 during Operation Grenade shortly after crossing the Roer river. The last soldier is carrying a M1A1 bazooka.

A BAR gunner of the 29th Division checks out a suspicious cellar in Julich during Operation Grenade on 23 February 1945. As will be noticed, BAR gunners carried a larger pouch to accommodate the bigger BAR magazines.

A wounded GI of the 102nd Division is carried out to an aid station by German prisoners of war on 23 February 1945 during Operation Grenade, the battle for the Roer dams. This was the first day of the offensive, and the division spent most of the day in a frustrating attempt to get bridges over the Roer river near Linnich, Germany.

A good character study of a GI from the 413th Infantry, 104th Division during the fighting in Mannheim, Germany on 27 February 1945, four days after having crossed the Roer river. He is wearing the M1928 haversack and is carrying two fragmentation hand grenades.

A 4.2 inch mortar provides fire support for Ninth Army operations near Baal, Germany on 24 February 1945 during Operation Grenade. These heavy mortars were not organic to infantry division, but were operated by Chemical Mortar Battalions (Motorized) originally to provide smoke during combat operations. Their heavy firepower potential led to changes and they were also regularly used to provide high explosive support as well.

A pair of M1 57mm anti-tank guns of the 29th Division are brought forward to provide fire support during the Ninth Army's attack on Rheydt, Germany on 1 March 1945. By this stage of the war, German armor was not often encountered, and the 57mm guns were used as direct fire support against bunkers and German field fortifications.

A squad from the 2nd Ranger Battalion prepare for a mission near Ruhrburg, Germany on 3 March 1945. The area had been the scene of intense fighting in February for the control of the Roer river dams, including the Paulushof regulating dam near Ruhrburg. Several of the GIs wear the Ranger flash on their shoulder, though it has been obscured by the censor.

Papers please! A GI inspects the pass of a German farmer near Bedersdorf on 12 March 1945. He is armed with a M1 carbine.

A machine gun team from the 65th Division moves forward near Buss, Germany on 20 March 1945. The machine-gunner in the center of the group is carrying the M1918A6 .30 cal light machine gun, a variant of the normal Browning light machine gun with a bipod and stock intended to make the weapon more mobile than the tripod mounted M1918A4.

GIs, probably from the 104th Division, cautiously advance through the rubble of Cologne. The majority of the city on the west bank of the Rhine was seized by the 3rd Armored Division and 104th Division in early March, but fighting continued along the river through March.

Another view of troops of the 65th Division moving through Buss on 20 March 1945, the day before they broke through the Siegfried line near Neunkirchen. This is a 60mm mortar team, with the GI in the center carrying the small mortar in the folded position. The GI behind him is wearing the M2 ammo pouch, a canvas saddlebag that carried mortar bombs in pockets on the front and back.

An 81mm mortar of the 417th Infantry, 76th Division fires during the fighting in Bacharach, Germany on 24 March 1945 in preparation to the Rhine crossing two days later. The ground to the left is covered with the black fiber-board containers in which the 81mm mortar bombs came packed.

Medics from the 92nd Cavalry Reconnaissance Squadron evacuate a wounded GI on a stretcher near Westernitz, Germany on 29 March 1945. The medics are wearing the standard helmet with Red Cross insignia and arms bands.

A medic from the 17th Airborne Division tends to a wounded paratrooper during Operation Varsity, the northern Rhine crossings on 31 March 1945. This was the last major airborne jump of the war in Europe.

A bazooka team from the 94th Division takes aim at a German position during the fighting near the Mannheim police station on 29 March 1945 after Patton's Third Army had pushed across the Rhine near Oppenheim a few days before. The GIs are wearing the M1943 field jackets and trousers, which by this stage of the campaign had become the most common battledress for infantry. The rifleman on the left is still wearing his overcoat.

A GI from the 65th Division takes a break near Katharinberg, Germany on 9 April 1945 with a newly found puppy in his lap. His Thompson .45 cal submachine gun has a double magazine, with a second magazine taped to the first to speed reloading.

Paratroopers of the XVIII Airborne Corps try out one of the new M18 57mm recoilless rifles during fighting around Munster in late March 1945. An initial batch of fifty of these were sent to the ETO in March 1945 along with training instructors, and they were used primarily by airborne units.